Cliff's Edge
A black comedy
Paul Beard

New Theatre Publications - London
www.plays4theatre.com

© 2013 BY Paul Beard

First published in 2001

The edition published in 2013

New Theatre Publications

2 Hereford Close | Warrington | Cheshire | WA1 4HR | 01925 485605

www.plays4theatre.com   email: info@plays4theatre.com

New Theatre Publications is the trading name of the publishing house that is owned by members of the Playwrights' Co-operative. This innovative project was launched on the 1st October 1997 by writers Paul Beard and Ian Hornby with the aim of encouraging the writing and promotion of the very best in New Theatre by Professional and Amateur writers for the Professional and Amateur Theatre at home and abroad.

ISBN 9 781 840 94930 8

Characters

Cliff
Gary
Sue

4

Copyright Information

The play is fully protected under the Copyright laws of the British Commonwealth of Nations, the United States of America and all countries of the Berne and Universal Copyright Conventions.

All rights including Stage, Motion Picture, Radio, television, Public Reading, and Translation into Foreign Languages, are strictly reserved.

No part of this publication may lawfully be reproduced in ANY form or by any means - photocopying, typescript, recording (including video-recording), manuscript, electronic, mechanical or otherwise - or be transmitted or stored in a retrieval system, without prior permission.

Licenses for amateur performances are issued subject to the understanding that it shall be made clear in all advertising matter that the audience will witness an amateur performance; that the names of the authors of the plays shall be included on all programmes, and that the integrity of the authors' work will be preserved.

The Royalty Fee is subject to contract and subject to variation at the sole discretion of New Theatre Publications.

In Theatres of Halls seating Four Hundred or more the fee will be subject to negotiation.

In Territories Overseas the fee quoted may not apply. A fee will be quoted on application to New Theatre Publications, London.

Video-Recording of Amateur Productions

Please note that the copyright laws governing video-recording are extremely complex and that it should not be assumed that any play may be video-recorded for whatever purpose without first obtaining the permission of the appropriate agents. The fact that a play is published by New Theatre Publications does not indicate that video rights are available or that New Theatre Publications control such rights.

Performing Licence Applications

A performing licence for these plays will be issued by "New Theatre Publications" subject to the following conditions.

Conditions

1. That the performance fee is paid in full on the date of application for a licence.
2. That the name of the author(s) is/are clearly shown in any programme or publicity material.
3. That the author(s) is/are entitled to receive two complimentary tickets to see his/her/their work in performance if they so wish.
4. That a copy of the play is purchased from New Theatre Publications for each named speaking part and a minimum of three copies purchased for backstage use.
5. That a copy of any review be forwarded to New Theatre Publications.
6. That the New Theatre Publications logo is clearly shown on any publicity material. This is available on our website.

Fees

Details of script prices and fees payable for each performance or public reading can be obtained by telephone to (+44) 01925 485605 or to the address below.

Alternatively, latest prices can be obtained from our website www.plays4theatre.com where credit/debit cards can be used for payment.

To apply for a performing licence for any play please write to New Theatre Publications 2 Hereford Close, Warrington, Cheshire WA1 4HR or email info@plays4theatre.com with the following details:-

1. Name and address of theatre company.
2. Details of venue including seating capacity.
3. Dates of proposed performance or public reading.
4. Contact telephone number for Author's complimentary tickets.

Or apply directly via our website at www.plays4theatre.com

Cliff's Edge
by
Paul Beard

Characters
Cliff
Gary
Sue

The cliff top at Beachy Head.

Gary, a man in his late 20's sits on a rock at the edge. He writes something on a notepad and places the pen and pad on the ground beside his left leg. He stares out to sea and is obviously depressed. Cliff, an older man enters up R. He stands besides Gary and takes a deep breath, savouring the ozone.

Cliff *(bright)* Is this Beachy Head?

Gary *(staring out, he sighs)* Yeah.

Cliff The place where people jump?

　　　(Pause.)

Gary *(staring out, thoughtful)* Possibly.

Cliff *(looking down)* Long way down, isn't it?

Gary *(staring out, he sighs)* Yeah.

Cliff Can't be easy identifying anyone after they've hit those.

Gary *(staring out, thoughtful)* No.

Cliff *(looking down)* Can't see anybody down there.

Gary *(staring out, he sighs)* I haven't looked.

Cliff *(looking along the coastline)* Definitely no-one there.

Gary Good.

　　　(Pause.)

Cliff Bet that water's cold.

Gary Probably.

Cliff I don't think I could jump.

Gary *(aside)* Pity.

Cliff I'm only trying to make conversation.

Gary Go away.

Cliff There's no need to be rude.

(Slight pause.)

Gary Sorry.

Cliff Just because you've got the raving hump it doesn't give you the right to be rude.

Gary *(sarcastic)* Please. I'd be eternally grateful if you could find it in your heart to leave. There. I'm being polite. Is that all right?

Cliff Still detect a touch of animosity in your voice.

Gary You're not going to go away whatever I say, are you?

Cliff It *is* a public footpath.

Gary I *was* here first.

Cliff *(sarcastic)* Oh, I see, there's a queue for that spot, is there?

(Pause.)

Gary No.

Cliff I'll just wait till you've finished then.

Gary I'd appreciate it if you didn't talk to me.

Cliff My lips are sealed.

Gary Thanks.

(Cliff takes a couple of strides away from Gary who stares out to sea. Short pause.)

Cliff It's really nice here.

Gary For God's sake!

Cliff What?

Gary Stop talking to me.

Cliff I wasn't.

Gary I don't see anybody else here.

Cliff I was merely remarking to myself what a nice place it is.

Gary You're doing it again.

Cliff What?

Gary Talking to me. Don't you understand? I want to be alone.

(Pause.)

Cliff Greta Garbo.

Gary Sorry?

Cliff I want to be alone. Greta Garbo. It's a line from one of her films.

Gary Hasta la vista, baby.

Cliff What?

Gary Arnold Schwarzenegger. It's one of his. Just before he picks somebody up and throws them off a cliff.

Cliff I'm only trying to help.

Gary I don't want your help. *(Pause.)* I came here to think.
(Pause.)

Cliff Not going to jump then?

Gary Sorry?

Cliff Jump. Geronimo and all that. I said to myself when I first saw you, there's a jumper if ever I saw one.

Gary So, you thought you'd do your good Samaritan bit and try and talk me out of it?

Cliff No, I thought I'd capture the moment on video and send it to "You've Been Framed".

Gary *(hurt)* You callous bastard.

Cliff *(smug)* I'd prefer entrepreneur.

Gary *(pleading)* Please go away.

Cliff Don't you want any company then?

Gary I don't want anything.

Cliff Cup of tea?

Gary Nothing.

Cliff Game of cards?

Gary For God's sake!

Cliff I'll wait over here then.

Gary Thanks. *(Cliff takes a few steps away from Gary. After a short pause, Cliff begins to whistle the funeral march.)* You're whistling.

Cliff One of my many talents.

Gary Please don't whistle.

Cliff Very comforting - whistling.

Gary Not for me.

Cliff I could change the tune if you like.

Gary I'd prefer it if you stopped altogether.

Cliff Enough said.

Gary Thanks. (*Short pause. Cliff begins to hum badly, 'Ode to Joy'.*) I don't believe this.

Cliff Now what's wrong?

Gary You're humming.

Cliff You don't like Beethoven?

Gary Beethoven by the L.S.O. I love. 'Ode to Joy' hummed in a range of different keys I can do without.

Cliff I try my best.

Gary Oh, you're very trying.

Cliff I'll shut up then, shall I?

Gary I'd appreciate it.

Cliff Total silence from now on.

Gary Thanks.

(*Long pause.*)

Cliff Do you want a cigarette?

Gary I've given up.

Cliff Recently?

Gary Three weeks, four days, seven hours, but who's counting?

Cliff Not a good idea giving up when you're manically depressed.

(*Pause.*)

Gary No.

Cliff Might as well have one. It's not going to kill you and it's a lot less painful than throwing yourself over the edge.

Gary Thanks.

Cliff Low tar.

Gary Very considerate.

Cliff 1.1mg of nicotine. Hardly seems worth the effort.

Gary You not having one?

Cliff Don't smoke. Never have. Filthy habit. Always carry a packet for emergencies like this though.

Gary Very thoughtful.

Cliff I like to think so.

Gary Do I get a light?

Cliff Haven't got one.

Gary Sorry?

Cliff I couldn't live with my conscience if I was instrumental in giving somebody lung cancer.

Gary I don't believe this.

Cliff Have you seen this Government warning? *(He reads.)* Smoking causes heart disease. That cigarette could have been your last.

Gary Chance would be a fine thing.

Cliff *(reading)* Never smoke whilst pregnant.

Gary I'll bear that in mind. *(Looks at his watch.)*

Cliff Nice watch. Shame to ruin it. It'll be smashed to smithereens or someone from the rescue service will probably nick it. Now, you don't strike me as the type of person that would want it to go to a complete stranger.

(During the speech Gary takes off his wrist watch.)

Gary *(handing his watch to Cliff)* Have it

Cliff *(disappointed)* It's a Timex.

Gary Yes.

Cliff I only caught sight of the 'X' on the dial. I thought it was a Rolex. You keep it. You can time how long it takes for anyone to get to you before you die. Then your next of kin can sue the rescue service under the Government charter if they're late.

Gary *(sad)* Haven't got a next of kin.

Cliff Hardly a reason to jump off a cliff.

Gary *(reluctant)* That's not the reason.

Cliff What is?

Gary *(embarrassed)* I'm an actor.

Cliff *(laughing)* What sort of answer is that? "I'm an actor." To jump or not to jump, that is the question. Once more onto the beach dear...

Gary ...all right. I'm a failed actor.

Cliff No you're not. I recognised you the minute you walked in the pub.

Gary *(unsure)* You recognised me?

Cliff You played Miss Diane's brother in 'Crossroads'.

Gary *(disbelief)* You're the first person that's recognised me in ten years.

Cliff *(hardly surprised)* Really?

Gary Apart from my agent. He still recognises me - occasionally.

Cliff Never missed an episode. Devastated, we were, when they took it off.

Gary We?

Cliff The wife. Great fan she was. Benny was her favourite.

Gary *(disappointed)* Oh.

Cliff Did he ever find that spanner?

Gary Sorry?

Cliff He went off to fetch a spanner and was never seen again.

Gary Probably couldn't find it.

Cliff Was he really that thick?

Gary It's called acting. It's what some of us do. When we're given the chance.

Cliff He was very good.

Gary I suppose you do a lot of this, do you?

Cliff What?

Gary Talk people out of jumping.

Cliff *(proud)* Good success rate so far.

Gary Really?

Cliff One in five's not bad.

Gary Not too good for the one that jumps.

Cliff *(embarrassed)* The other way round.

Gary Sorry?

Cliff Save one and four jump.

Gary Oh.

Cliff I'm still perfecting my technique. Just a matter of finding the right approach. Get to meet all sorts in the pub game. Have to know how to talk to people or you'd never survive.

Gary What if I never came in the pub?

Cliff Always come in the pub first. Spot them a mile off. Buy one drink, sit on their own till last orders, then take the slow walk down here to make the final decision.

Gary You recognised me. I still can't believe it. I haven't worked since 'Crossroads'.

Cliff Really?

Gary Plenty of work before that. Played Lear at Stratford, got rave reviews for my Bottom at the Old Vic. Had some wonderful parts, before that offer of security came along. Soap. It makes you, then breaks you. *(Pause.)* I'd given up on ever being recognised again. *(Pause.)* Thanks.

Cliff The locals call this place 'Cliff's edge' - after me. In honour of all the lives I've saved. There was talk at one stage of a porcelain plaque being placed here.

Gary That's nice.

Cliff Bit of a problem with the town council though.

Gary Hardly an eyesore.

Cliff Worried that somebody might trip over it and go over the edge.

Gary Got a point I suppose. *(He extends his hand towards Cliff to shake)* Thanks - Cliff.

Cliff *(shaking his hand)* It's Harry.

Gary Sorry?

Cliff Harry Webb. That's why they call me Cliff.

Gary *(unsure)* Oh.

Cliff What's your name then?

Gary Gary.

Cliff Good name for an actor that.

Gary Really?

Cliff Solid British name.

Gary Name one famous actor called Gary.

Cliff Well, there's always got to be a first. Perhaps you should adopt a stage name.

Gary That is my stage name.

Cliff Use your own then.

Gary Lawrence Olivier?

Cliff You'd probably get more work.

Gary *(laughing)* Knowing my luck, I'd end up with third spear carrier from the left.

Cliff Well, you seemed to have cheered up. Here, this'll make you laugh. When you throw yourself over a cliff, what's the last thing that goes through your mind?

Gary Go on.

Cliff Your arse. *(He laughs at his own joke.)* Do you get it? Your arse goes through your mind as you hit the deck. *(Now in hysterical laughter.)* Oh God, that is such a good joke.

Gary Have you told it to any other potential suicides?

Cliff *(controlling himself)* No, I only heard it last week. Did I tell it right?

Gary I wouldn't give up your day job.

Cliff That's a piece of professional advice, is it?

Gary *(proud)* I am a professional, aren't I? *(Over dramatic)* I - am - an - actor.

Cliff Of course you are.

Gary They used to queue outside the studios to take my picture. Women would offer themselves to me and send me their underwear and all because my face would appear on the little screen in the corner of their room. It didn't matter that we were all speaking a load of old drivel. We were stars. Now? Nothing. *(Pause.)* Would you like an autograph?

Cliff What?

Gary Please. It's been such a long time.

Cliff Go on then if it'll make you happy. Got a pen?

Gary *(moves his hand slightly towards his pen and then quickly retracts.)* No.

Cliff I'll nip back to the pub and get one.

Gary *(sad)* I'll never forget you for this.

Cliff *(unsure)* You will be all right, won't you?

Gary *(smiling but sad)* You saved my life. You recognised me.

Cliff Back in a tick.

(Cliff exits up R. Gary sits on the rock and stares out to sea momentarily. He picks up the pad and stares at what he has written. He stands and walks to the edge carrying the notepad. He places the pad on the ground and gives his finest performance, out to sea. Unseen by him Sue enters up L. Her arm is in a plaster cast.)

Gary Be absolute for death: either death or life shall thereby be the sweeter. Reason thus with life: If I do lose thee, I do lose a thing

Sue Care in the community, is it?

Gary I'm an actor.

Sue *(pointing to pad)* Suicide note, is it?

Gary Sorry?

Sue Going to jump, are you?

Gary No.

Sue Might as well, you're a lousy actor.

Gary Thanks.

Sue You're in the wrong place if you're going to jump. This bit's for cars. If you jumped off here you'd only land on the ledge. Probably break an arm or a leg or something, but that's all.

Gary I'm not going to jump.

Sue Well, if you change your mind the best spot's over there. *(Indicating right.)* Sheer drop. Shallow water. Wouldn't stand a chance. If you want to drive over the edge it depends on the size of your car as to which is the best spot. This is good for a large saloon. Metro or smaller, *(Indicating left.)* you need to go over there.

Gary I'm not going to jump.

Sue Depressed, aren't you?

Gary I was just feeling sorry for myself. That's all. I realise that now.

Sue Might as well get it over and done with. Bit pointless coming down here and not going through with it.

Gary I've changed my mind.

Sue You can't. That's the funny thing about depression.

Gary Hardly funny.

Sue My psychiatrist says it's a chemical imbalance. If you don't get the right cocktail of drugs to correct it, you might as well slit your wrists and be done with it. What are you on?

Gary Nothing

Sue There you go then. You'll do it sooner or later. It's only a matter of time. I'll give you a shove if you like.

Gary I don't want to die.

Sue Oh, I see. Cry for help, is it? No good jumping if it's a cry for help.

Too risky. Pills are best for a cry for help. Not paracetamols, mind. Do too much internal damage with those. I find Mogadon are the best. That way at least you get a good night's sleep out of it.

Gary Bit of an expert, are you?

Sue Tried hanging myself once. Didn't tie the knot properly. Got a nasty rope burn though, had to wear a scarf for nearly two months.

Gary Sounds painful.

Sue Did the trick mind. Got three weeks away from the old man and kids with that one.

Gary Kids?

Sue Four. First at fifteen, father did a bunk. Twins at seventeen, one night stand, father unknown. Lost one at nineteen, just as well, married man. Last one popped out two months ago, father possibly a Greek waiter or an Indian cab driver - dark skinned.

Gary I thought you said you were married?

Sue Lost his tackle in a boating accident. Tragic really. Makes a wonderful father.

Gary Have you found out what's causing it yet?

Sue I expect it's the sex.

Gary The depression.

Sue Doctor says it's post-natal, but what do they know?

Gary A bit more than you and me.

Sue I didn't have a problem until I saw the doctor. I only went over to have some stitches out of my wrist. He took one look and referred me to a psychiatrist.

Gary You slit your wrist?

Sue It was an accident. I was helping to build a greenhouse and cut it on one of the panes of glass.

Gary Why didn't you tell him?

Sue I didn't get a chance. I showed him my wrist, mentioned depression and the next thing I know I'm sitting in a cottage hospital listening to piped whale music and being prescribed an assortment of different coloured pills.

Gary So you were depressed?

Sue No, I was asking for my husband. He'd been feeling down on account of his lack of sexual activity.

Gary You should have said something.

Sue I didn't like to. They all seemed so caring.

Gary Well, you shouldn't have taken the tablets then.

Sue Are you kidding? £15.75 they cost. I couldn't afford to just throw them away.

Gary You're mad.

Sue I am now. It's official. Manically depressed. It's written on my notes. One minute I'm up the next minute I'm down.

Gary I get a bit like that sometimes.

Sue Of course you do. You're depressed.

Gary No. I'm just a bit down, that's all.

Sue Can't sleep?

Gary Not recently.

Sue Off your food?

Gary Can't remember the last time I had a proper sit down meal.

Sue Can't get an erection?

Gary Haven't tried. Can't be bothered.

Sue Can't be bothered. Classic sign. You are definitely depressed.

Gary All right, I admit, I was a bit depressed, but then I met Cliff.

Sue He's very good, isn't he?

Gary You've met him?

Sue No, but I've got an original copy of Living Doll. I went off him when he went all religious.

Gary Not that Cliff. The guy from the pub over there.

Sue Don't go in pubs. Alcohol's a depressant.

Gary You should speak to him. He could help you.

Sue I don't need any help. I only came down here because my plaster's due off tomorrow. I thought I'd go for a leg this time. Get a bit more sympathy on crutches.

Gary You're going to jump?

Sue Only here. It's OK. I'll land on the ledge. I know what I'm doing.

Gary Please don't jump.

Sue Did you want to go first?

Gary I can't.

Sue Are you queer?

Gary No.

Sue Most of them are though, aren't they? Actors?

Gary No more than traffic wardens I should think.

Sue Traffic wardens? Probably a uniform thing.

Gary That's not what I meant.

(Pause.)

Sue Do you fancy a shag?

Gary No.

Sue You are queer.

Gary I'm not.

Sue Don't you fancy me?

Gary No.

Sue There's no shame in being a homosexual these days. In Brighton it's almost compulsory. That could be your problem. You should come out. You'll feel a lot better. It's probably deep rooted in your sub-conscience.

Gary Why am I listening to you? You're mad.

Sue The last bloke who jumped off here was a homosexual.

Gary I don't want to know.

Sue Broke both legs. Don't think he was a traffic warden though.

Gary You're mad.

Sue You wouldn't be the first actor to jump off here.

Gary I'm not going to jump.

Sue Had a bloke from 'East-enders' jump once.

Gary *(sarcastic)* Hardly jump twice, would he.

Sue Swapped him for a different actor a couple of weeks later. Didn't look nothing like the first one. They do a lot of that don't they?

Gary Watch a lot of T.V, do you?

Sue Loads. Never seen you though. You couldn't have been that good.

Gary I was in "Crossroads".

Sue No wonder you're depressed.

Gary I'm depressed because I haven't worked since.

Sue At least you can admit you're depressed now. It took me ages to finally admit it.

Gary Have you actually ever tried to kill yourself?

Sue I laid on the railway line for about three hours once.

Gary So you have?

Sue I made sure they were on strike first. Cry for help see. That's the difference between you and me. You want to die and I'm just looking for love and attention.

Gary Nobody wants to die.

Sue They don't come down here for flying lessons.

Gary No.

Sue It's very hard, don't you think? Throwing yourself off a cliff . It's not as if you can change your mind half way down, is it?

Gary You pass out. On the way down. You don't feel a thing.

Sue Apparently, there was a pilot once who fell a mile and half without a parachute into a snow drift.

Gary And you're going to tell me he never passed out, right?

Sue No. He died.

Gary Did they find out why he jumped without a parachute?

Sue Probably a traffic warden.

Gary *(thoughtful)* Possibly.

Sue It's not easy, is it? Killing yourself.

Gary It used to be a criminal offence to commit suicide.

Sue Bit pointless prosecuting a corpse.

Gary No, if you died you were all right. It's only if you survived you ended up at the Old Bailey.

Sue Typical. Just when you're at your lowest ebb they throw you in jail. Life can be very cruel, don't you think?

Gary I've got an audition for a voice-over tomorrow. Cadbury's fruit and Nut advert. Probably won't get it. Not very good at squirrel impersonations.

Sue I can do a great frog.

Gary I'd better go. I'll miss the next train otherwise.

Sue Are you going to catch it, or jump in front of it?

(Pause.)

Gary Who knows?

Sue Don't forget to shout "Geronimo". It helps, apparently.

Gary I'll bear it in mind. *(Exits up R.)*

Sue *(calling after him)* Good luck. *(Pause.)* Au revoir. *(Pause.)* Bon voyage.

Gary *(offstage and fading away) GERONIMO!*

(Pause.)

Sue What a pratt. *(She walks to the edge and looks over.)* Sheer drop. No ledge. Perfect. *(She picks up the pen and pad and writes something. She reads.)* "Goodbye". That about says it all. *(She adds something to the note and reads.)* "Kiss, kiss, kiss". Nice touch that. *(She puts the pen and pad down and walks to the edge.)*

Cliff *(enters up R)* Where is he?

Sue Who?

Cliff The actor.

Sue He jumped.

Cliff But I've got the pen.

Sue Not a lot of use to him now. The current's coming this way, he should be floating past in a couple of minutes you could throw it down to him.

Cliff What did he go and jump for?

Sue He was depressed.

Cliff He's the third this week.

Sue There's a lot of it about.

Cliff You just can't help some people.

Sue Strange bloke. He thought that all traffic wardens were homosexuals.

Cliff He was in 'Crossroads'.

Sue So he said.

Cliff Such a waste of talent.

Sue He was crap. I caught him reciting Shakespeare. Very bad Shakespeare.

Cliff Bit off an expert, are you?

Sue Studied at R.A.D.A. Got a B.A in Theatre Studies.

Cliff Bachelor of Arts. I'm impressed.

Sue B.A. Bloody awful. I'm also a compulsive liar.

Cliff Are you?

Sue I just said so.

Cliff Ah, but were you lying?

Sue I wouldn't know the truth if it hit me in the face. My therapist says it's because I was bottle fed as a baby. Mum got milk fever. Nipples were too small. Like puppy dogs' noses, apparently.

Cliff Is that the truth?

Sue No, I made it up. Sorry. I can't help it.

Cliff Are you thinking of jumping?

Sue Why?

Cliff I haven't managed to save one person this week. To tell you the truth it's beginning to get me down.

Sue Are you the guy from the pub?

Cliff Yes.

Sue What's it called?

Cliff The Beachy Head.

Sue Not very original.

Cliff Not very busy either. No regulars see? Mainly passing trade.

Sue And those that do pass come straight down here I suppose.

Cliff Exactly.

Sue Silly place for a pub if you ask me.

Cliff It was the wife's idea. She wanted a pub in the country. We sunk our entire life savings into the place. Bit of a disaster really.

Sue It's only money. At least you've got each other.

Cliff She's having an affair with the rep' for pickled eggs.

Sue How do you know?

Cliff She's started using excess amounts of Lavender Toilet Water to disguise the smell of the vinegar.

Sue Have you talked to her about it?

Cliff We don't talk. That's one of the reasons why I come down here. It's easier to talk to strangers.

Sue Is it the first time she's had an affair?

Cliff She was married when I met her. I suppose I should have recognised the signs. There's not many women that allow full carnal knowledge on the first date. Not for the cost of a Babycham and a packet of Cheese and Onion crisps anyway.

Sue   I don't like Cheese and Onion crisps.

Cliff   Are you married?

Sue   Divorced. I came home one day and found him wearing my best ra-ra skirt, stockings, suspenders and wellington boots. He's living with a hairdresser in Bognor Regis now.

Cliff   What's she like?

Sue   His name's Simon.

Cliff   Your ex-husband?

Sue   The bloke he lives with.

Cliff   Oh. Sorry.

Sue   I wouldn't have minded so much if it was another woman.

Cliff   Any kids?

Sue   No, my fallopian tubes are twisted. Saves a fortune on contraception.

Cliff   Every cloud has a silver lining.

Sue   You look really fed up.

Cliff   *(looking over the edge)* That water looks very inviting.

Sue   Hardly. It's almost raw sewerage. If you survived the fall you'd probably die of gastro-enteritis.

Cliff   Were you thinking of jumping?

Sue   Why? Do you want to save me?

Cliff   I'd give it my best shot.

Sue   Go on then. If it'll cheer you up.

      (Pause.)

Cliff   Please don't jump.

Sue   Was that it? Your best shot?

Cliff   It doesn't work because we've already met.

Sue   Try meeting again then.

Cliff   No, it wouldn't work.

Sue   Of course it would. I'm schizophrenic. You wouldn't even know it's me.

Cliff   OK then. *(Walks a few steps away; returns.)* It's nice here, isn't it?

Sue   Piss off.

Cliff What?

Sue Are you deaf?

Cliff No.

Sue Then piss off.

Cliff I think I preferred the other you.

Sue Do I know you?

Cliff It's Cliff.

Sue You don't look nothing like him.

Cliff From the pub.

Sue Given up on The Shadows then?

Cliff I think I'm giving up on you.

Sue Don't you love me anymore?

Cliff What?

Sue I can sue you for breach of promise, you know.

Cliff I didn't promise you anything.

Sue You're all the same. Men. It's at times like these I'm glad I'm a lesbian.

Cliff Are you?

Sue Is it Wednesday?

Cliff Friday.

Sue It's no then. I'm only a lesbian on Wednesdays.

Cliff I'm confused now.

Sue I get confused on Sundays. Mondays I play scrum half for the All-Blacks.

Cliff You're mad.

Sue You wanted to play this stupid game.

Cliff You might as well jump. I think you're past saving.

Sue I might be mad, but I'm not stupid enough to jump. I've got a family to consider.

Cliff I thought you said you couldn't have children?

Sue That was her. There's nothing wrong with my internals.

Cliff Only your brain.

Sue Are you taking the piss?

Cliff I wouldn't dare.

Sue I have been known to have psychopathic tendencies.

Cliff You do seem a little aggressive.

Sue Aggressive? This is me being nice. You'll know it when I get aggressive.

Cliff How?

Sue My teeth will be sunk into your gonads.

Cliff *(stepping back)* I think I prefer you being nice.

Sue My analyst says it's a deep-seated aversion to oral sex that makes me aim for a man's nether region.

Cliff Really?

Sue Are you in therapy?

Cliff Not yet.

Sue You should try it.

Cliff Doesn't seem to have done you much good.

Sue You should have seen me before I found myself. The real me.

Cliff Are you real now?

Sue I'm not a mirage. Touch me. I won't go pop.

Cliff OK. *(Reaches out and touches her arm.)*

Sue RAPE! RAPE!

Cliff *(panicking)* I didn't touch you. Well, I did, but I didn't if you know what I mean. It's just that...

Sue Calm down. I'm in the neighbourhood watch. You can't be too relaxed with crime prevention that's all.

Cliff I was really worried then.

Sue Prevention is better than the cure, isn't that what they say?

Cliff In your case I'm not so sure.

Sue You're supposed to be nice to me if you intend to stop me from jumping.

Cliff The way I feel at the moment I'll probably join you.

Sue I don't need any encouragement.

Cliff Sorry. It's just that the pickled egg rep's due later.

Sue More lavender water eh?

Cliff They both get up my nose.

Sue   You should try getting some help if you're feeling that bad.

Cliff   Is that your note pad down there?

Sue   It belonged to your actor friend.

Cliff   *(picks up the notepad and reads.)*"Goodbye. Kiss, kiss, kiss."

Sue   Says it all, don't you think?

Cliff   A man of few words our actor.

Sue   I'll never forget the last thing he said.

Cliff   What was it?

Sue   "GERONIMO"!

Cliff   That's not funny.

Sue   You've got to laugh haven't you? Otherwise you'd go mad.

Cliff   It's too late for you then.

Sue   Far too late. *(Walks closer to the edge.)* See you on the other side.

Cliff   Wait!

Sue   What for?

Cliff   You can't jump.

Sue   Why not?

Cliff   What about me?

Sue   Sorry, did you want to go first?

Cliff   I can't lose two in one day.

Sue   Why?

Cliff   It'll ruin my averages for a start.

Sue   That's a bit selfish, isn't it?

Cliff   Can't you do it tomorrow?

Sue   I might not feel like it tomorrow.

Cliff   You won't know if you jump now.

Sue   True.

Cliff   You might be happy tomorrow.

Sue   Do you think so?

Cliff   It's possible.

Sue   Then again, if I'm not I've wasted another whole day.

Cliff   Not wasted. You've really helped me.

Sue   How?

Cliff   Shoulder to cry on and all that.

Sue   You didn't cry.

Cliff   I might yet.

Sue   I've never been wanted before.

Cliff   Come away from the edge. Please.

Sue   Go on then.

Cliff   What?

Sue   Cry.

Cliff   I can't.

Sue   Why not?

Cliff   I haven't got anything to cry about.

Sue   Your wife's knocking off the pickled egg salesman, your business is going to the wall and you've talked a talented actor into committing suicide and you say you've got nothing to cry about?

Cliff   You're right. *(Begins to falsely cry.)*

Sue   That's not very convincing.

Cliff   *(crying louder)* I'm trying, I'm trying.

Sue   *(stepping back)* All right, all right, I'm not going to jump.

Cliff   *(sobbing gently getting under control)* Promise?

Sue   Promise.

Cliff   Works every time.

Sue   What does?

Cliff   The crying routine. If all else fails, burst into tears and it'd even stop a lemming from jumping.

Sue   You're good at this, aren't you?

Cliff   Just a matter of finding the right approach.

Sue   I'll have to be going now.

Cliff   You're not going to…

Sue   …No. Not today anyway.

Cliff   Thanks. I don't think I could handle losing two in one day.

Sue   I'd better go. They lock the door of the hospital at five. Keeps all the nutters out.

Cliff   See you tomorrow, perhaps?

Sue You'll have to find a new approach. I won't fall for that one again.

Cliff Count on it. *(Sue exits up R.. Cliff calls after her.)* Three o'clock. After closing time.

Sue *(offstage and fading away)* GERONIMO!

Cliff Bitch. *(Cliff picks up the notepad and rips out the page and throws it to the floor. He quickly scribbles something and puts the pad down on the floor. He walks slowly to the edge, looks down and pauses.)* What's the name of that bloody Indian?

(Blackout. End)

Other NTP Plays by Paul Beard

Come the Resolution

Death of a Clown

Lavender Years

Piste Off

Shadows In Red

Strangeways

Swingers

Waiting for Pierrepoint

Broadway to Hollywood & Back

Dying for Dinner

Robin Hoodlum

The only
monthly magazine
passionate
about
amateur theatre

www.ingramcontent.com/pod-product-compliance
Lightning Source LLC
Chambersburg PA
CBHW060606030426
42337CB00019B/3629